They Don't Make 'Em Like That Any More

A Picture-History of Canadian Cars 1932-47

by John de Bondt

Copyright © 1987 by John de Bondt

All rights reserved: no part of this book may be reproduced in any form or by any means, electronic or mechanical, except by a reviewer, who may quote brief passages to be printed in a newspaper or magazine or broadcast on radio or television.

ISBN 0 88750 652 6

Typesetting and design by Michael Macklem

Printed in Canada

PUBLISHED IN CANADA BY OBERON PRESS

SURVIVAL AVENUE

From the very beginning, Canada has been a car-building nation, and here as elsewhere the motor industry has long been the motor of industry. Never was this more true than during the depression of the thirties, when Canadians needed cars but couldn't afford to buy them, and massive layoffs in automotive plants caused unemployment in hundreds of associated businesses.

Of course, there were by that time no really Canadian cars on the market. The era of tinkering and small-plant pioneering was long since over, research and development had become both essential and very expensive and the new and sophisticated manufacturing procedures required huge capital investments. A country like Canada, with a relatively small population, simply could not—and still cannot—support a fully developed automotive industry. Even in the United States—the home of the automobile—scores of well known cars had failed to survive the twenties. The casualties included such old and respected makes as Apperson, Chalmers, Cole, Haynes, Locomobile, Maxwell, Overland, Paige, Velie, Winton and others.

In the early thirties several more venerable marques joined the list, including the Auburn-Cord-Duesenberg trio as well as Durant, Essex, Franklin, Gardner, Jordan, Kissel, Marmon, Oakland, Peerless, Pierce-Arrow, Reo, Stearns-Knight and Stutz. With such a mortality rate south of the border, it's a wonder that any of the Canadian plants survived at all.

They did though, thanks in part to a protectionist tariff policy. There had been a 35% duty on imported carriages ever since Confederation (and before); a similar duty was levied on imported cars, though it was reduced to 30% in 1906. There had always, however, been a lower rate of duty on automotive parts, and this made it attractive for foreign companies to assemble or manufacture their cars in this country, although it did nothing to protect domestic car-makers from the competition of American-owned branch-plants.

From the outset, English cars had been permitted entry at preferential rates, in return for the similar treatment of Canadian vehicles in Britain and the Commonwealth. This arrangement provided an ideal investment climate for the American car-makers who, by establishing plants in Canada, could avoid our import duties and at the same time gain unrestricted access to the Commonwealth market.

The tariffs may have protected local industry, but of course they also made for higher prices in Canada. In 1926 public clamour over this difference in price led to the lowering of the duty on finished vehicles to just 20% on cars costing less than $1200 and $27\frac{1}{2}\%$ on those that cost more than that. To save the Canadian industry from total collapse, a rebate of 25% was applied to duties on parts, provided they were used in the manufacture of cars with a Canadian content of at least 50%.

By 1931, at the bottom of the depression, production had dropped to 83,000 vehicles from 263,000 in 1929. "The automobile industry," observed the Canadian Bank of Commerce, as it then was, in its monthly newsletter, "has been one of the most sorely affected by the depression." Increased tariffs were demanded. The importation of used cars was prohibited, as it still is, and the duty on new cars was raised once again to 30% for cars costing up to $2100 and 40% on higher-priced models. Packard and Pierce-Arrow, both makers of luxury cars, immediately opened plants in Canada.

In the next year, the duty on cars imported from Great Britain was eliminated. Fears that Austins and Morrises would flood the Canadian market proved groundless, since Canadians still tended to prefer American cars to the smaller overseas products.

In Europe, at this time, people regarded a motor-car as a luxury, something you could very well do without in hard times, but most Canadians, like their American neighbours, had by now become accustomed to cars as part of their way of life, as central to their mobility as trains in Europe or donkeys in Mexico. During the depression thousands of Canadians roamed the country looking for jobs. Some boarded freight trains; others, too broke to buy gasoline, used a Bennett Buggy—a horse-drawn automobile named after the Prime Minister of the day. But all over the country there were people searching for work in cars—old and rickety, perhaps, but private, motorized transportation nonetheless. Will Rogers' famous remark about America being the first nation ever to go to the poor-house in an automobile applied equally well to Canada.

But if Canadians needed cars now more than ever, they could hardly afford to buy a new one every four or five years. This led automakers to take drastic steps to reduce competition from used cars. Their solution: destroy them. General Motors actually paid its dealers $30 for every car they demolished. On 13 February, 1933, for example, a GM dealer in Winchester, Ontario filled out a "Used Car Disposal Report" (Form No. CO 23 5M-2-32 AP 8925) addressed to General Motors Products of Canada. "Please be advised," the report said, "that I have destroyed the undermentioned Used Cars, under your Used Car Disposal Plan. There is no lien or other encumbrance against any of the cars listed below."

The cars listed by the dealer included a Briscoe Touring Model 434, no model-year given, "Amount Allowed by Dealer: $40. Used Car Disposal Payment: $30." The Briscoe was built in Brockville, Ontario from 1916 until 1921. The other cars on this particular report were two 1919 Model T Fords, taken in at $30 each. "This is to certify," a statement at the bottom declared, "that I have personally seen the above-mentioned cars destroyed as per instructions in the following manner—starting motor, generator, carburetor, intake and exhaust manifolds smashed. The cylinder head and cylinder block broken. Hole knocked in radiator and instrument board destroyed, also headlamps. Grease plug on rear axle smashed in."

This graphic eyewitness account was to be signed by the Factory Representative, after which the Zone Manager would sign a memo to the Accounting Department: "This will be your authorization to issue cheque to the above-mentioned dealer for the above-mentioned cars at $30 per car." The first two copies were for the Zone Office; the third went to the dealer and the representative who had "personally seen" the massacre kept the fourth copy.

Car-makers also encouraged buyers by appealing to their sense of duty. Magazines such as *Maclean's* and *Saturday Night* duly echoed the sentiments of the industry in article after article pointing out the positive ripple effect of increased employment in automobile manufacturing. In an article published in 1936, *Maclean's* enlarged upon the number of plants, the number of workers employed and the aggregate wages paid in each of the provinces by makers of cars and parts for cars. Readers were admonished to "think of these things when you look at the new cars on display this month. Those who buy them will be doing more than making an investment in comfort and convenience and family transportation. You will be keeping a lot of dollar bills in circulation."

Apparently the thought that part of each such dollar would end up in the pockets of the parent firms south of the border was fairly widespread, and manufacturers took pains to make Canadians aware of the Canadian content in their products. "The increase in the technical ability of the local Canadian parts manufacturer has been a very marked factor in the last two or three years," wrote Major Eric Harris, manager of Electric Auto-Lite Ltd. of Sarnia in *Saturday Night* in 1931. "Every month that passes sees those cars that are manufactured in Canada become more and more complete Canadian cars."

Besides, as Beverley Owens argued the next year in *Maclean's*, "a great many Canadians hold stock in these American corporations, in addition to having a direct interest in the Canadian subsidiary plants; in fact, it is easily con-

The 1932 McLaughlin-Buick (right), like most cars of that year, was lovely to look at, but its straight-up radiator, open fenders and exposed horns would make it look hopelessly out-of-date a year later.

Do you know this
NEW MOTORING THRILL?

WITH the introduction of the new McLaughlin-Buick Eights for 1932, a different kind of motoring is here.

There's a new driving thrill in McLaughlin-Buick's *Wizard Control*, enabling you to change gears expertly and silently without using the clutch ... to change instantaneously from Conventional Drive to Free Wheeling and vice versa without reaching for controls ... and to accelerate, quietly, up to 40 miles per hour or more in second.

There's a new thrill in McLaughlin-Buick's High Compression, Valve-in-Head Engine, for it has more power, speed and acceleration.

There's new motoring comfort in these cars, for the *Ride Regulator* permits you instantly to adjust shock absorbers to any needs.

To know the thrill of the new McLaughlin-Buick you *must* drive it. The nearest dealer (find his location in your telephone book under the heading "General Motors Cars") has a car at your disposal. Drive it today!

∽ ∽ ∽

There are 34 models of the new McLaughlin-Buick Eights, priced from $1290, to $2870, at factory, Oshawa, Taxes extra.

The New
McLAUGHLIN-BUICK EIGHTS

Produced in Canada

FOR A QUARTER CENTURY — CANADA'S STANDARD CAR

ceivable that the total amount of Canadian money invested in the motor-car industry in general on this continent exceeds the amount invested in Canadian motor-car enterprises. So, while the larger share of profits arising from the sale of a Canadian-made car goes to pay dividends to American investors, that amount is offset by the Canadian investors' share, plus the financial return to Canadians out of the purchase of cars by Americans in their own country."

The argument was pointless, for there were no profits. The big Canadian car-makers were losing an average of $103 on every car they built in 1932!

Manufacturers minced no words in voicing their need for tariff protection. "Undoubtedly," wrote Florian Leduc, general sales manager for Willys-Overland, with evident satisfaction, "the new tariff scale on imported cars recently put into effect by the federal government will give the Canadian manufacturer of automobiles an impetus which will help materially in the general welfare not only of our particular industry but also of business prospects in general."

The president of Chrysler Corporation of Canada, J.D. Mansfield, had this to say: our existing industries "have developed in the main under a system of moderate tariff protection. Because of this tariff policy, vast investments have been made and factories established which furnish a livelihood for hundreds of thousands of Canadian families."

And for those who were still worried about the limited Canadian content in cars made in this country, R.S. McLaughlin, then president of General Motors of Canada, had these stern words: "Only if our market is broadened and a production volume attained that a stable protective tariff would give, can we work up ultimately to a higher percentage."

By 1934 the industry was in the black again and the next year production reached 173,000 vehicles. By 1936 Canadians were once again complaining about the high price-tags they saw in Canadian showrooms. Under the reciprocity agreement reached in that year, the duty on im-

This photograph by Margaret Bourke-White perfectly captures the geometrical beauty of the 1932 Hupmobile. This model won two Concours d'élégance medals in France, competing against the finest and costliest cars Europe had to offer—all at a price many Canadians could afford to pay. Hupmobiles were built in Windsor until 1936.

ported cars was reduced to 17½%. The national policy on Canadian content was extended in such a way as to allow manufacturers to import parts that were not available in Canada while obliging them to buy enough components in this country to maintain a minimum standard of Canadian content. One immediate effect was that Studebaker, a low-volume producer, ceased making cars in Canada; about the same time, General Motors began importing Cadillacs instead of making them here. The cheapest Cadillac cost $2081 in Canada, $636 more than in the US. But the company used exactly the same advertising artwork in both countries and didn't even bother to hide the Michigan licence-plates in ads that appeared in Canadian magazines.

In the late thirties the Canadian car industry enjoyed a tremendous growth in both capital investment and employment. When war broke out the industry became an integral part of the Allied war effort, and by 1940 Canadian carmakers were paying $20 million a year in wages to 15,000 employees. An equal number were employed in the manufacture of automotive parts; an additional 21,000 were employed in distribution, sales and service. "Perhaps," as C. D. Howe claimed in the House of Commons, "there is no country in the world producing automotive equipment in the volume that now obtains in Canada." The industry kept turning out passenger cars until 1942, though new ex-

In 1932 Graham set the styling pace for the entire industry with this curvaceous model (above) and no further changes were introduced until 1935. Grahams were made in Walkerville until 1940. Chevrolet (right) was the cheapest fullsize car on the Canadian market in 1933–a six for $660, $25 less than a four-cylinder Ford and $85 less than a Ford V-8. The sidemounts were optional at extra cost.

cise taxes were imposed by the federal government to curtail demand.

Year in and year out, Canadian auto-workers made good money, compared to their contemporaries in other industries. In 1935, for instance, wages in car plants averaged $1321 per year compared to $874 in the manufacturing industry in general.. By that time, wages were down almost 25% from the level reached in 1928, but real earnings, because of the decline in the cost of living, were higher than they had ever been.

What kind of cars did they build, these Canadians lucky enough to be on the assembly line instead of the bread-line? While the Europeans (nobody at that time had ever heard of Japanese cars) were building sports models, winning races and translating their experience into exciting designs for family cars with four-wheel independent suspension, front-wheel drive, torsion bars, light-weight frames and lower centres

How to save money
And Go Places in Style

HERE is Canada's golden rule for smart and thrifty motoring! Just step into any new Chevrolet Six— press down on that amazing Starterator—and go!

You can sweep past traffic in Chevrolet's silent second with never a disturbing sound. You can shift gears without even a click. You can relax, rested and cool, in Chevrolet's roomy, deep-cushioned closed Fisher bodies with No-Draft Ventilation. You can relax mentally, thanks to Safety Glass in windshield and ventilators and added quality throughout the car. And how a Chevrolet hugs the road, rides the rough spots and catches the eye of everyone who loves the new and smart!

But that's just a start. Half the thrill of owning this car is the way it saves you money. On purchase price— by offering you the lowest-priced, full-size, closed Six you can buy! And every mile you drive, because Chevrolet costs you *less* for gas, oil and upkeep—and has the best reputation of any low-priced car for freedom from repairs.

Considering both the pleasure side and the practical side—can you imagine a *better buy* than a Chevrolet Six, Canada's leader in sales!

CHEVROLET

STANDARD SIX   **MASTER SIX**

of gravity, Windsor, Walkervile and Oshawa kept toeing the Detroit line, with cavernous bodies, bulbous fenders and indifferent steering. Yet the Big Three—as well as Packards, Hudsons, Nashes and Studebakers—were seen all over the world, from Brussels to Batavia, for they were roomy and comfortable, silent and trouble-free.

Like artists, who sometimes do their best work when they're hungry, the car-makers turned out some of their most memorable vehicles during the depression. In 1932 the depression was at its worst, yet General Motors and Chrysler both turned out the most elegant, the most perfectly proportioned cars ever built, before or since. That same year, Ford startled the world with a smooth-running eight-cylinder engine in one of the industry's least expensive cars, while the small Graham company turned out a streamlined, fender-skirted model that set

the styling trend for the whole industry and changed the shape of cars forever. The fender skirts hid the mud-caked underbody that had until then been visible behind the wheels on all cars. Graham's radiator was clad in a graciously curved, heart-shaped chrome shell. Tootsie Toys promptly issed a complete line of 1/43-scale diecast sedans, coupés and convertibles based on the Graham and the car became a familiar object in thousands of boys' rooms all across the

What could be more evocative of the thirties than this 1933 Oldsmomile ad, with its rakish fashions and naively modern buildings? The Science Hall at left could have been built by Mussolini or Hitler. Both models offered, according to the manufacturers, a unique combination of style, performance, durability and low price—$845 for the eight, $745 for the six.

country. All automakers put fender skirts and slanted radiator shells on their cars the next year, and the boxy shape of the twenties became a thing of the past.

In the next six or seven years cars underwent greater and more dramatic changes in appearance than in any other comparable period. A car built in 1931 looks very much like a car built in the mid-teens, but by 1937 cars had ceased to look like a box on wheels and had acquired aerodynamic styling that expressed its function as a moving machine, like a bird or a fish. Detractors call this the melting-brick-of-ice-cream school of design, but the silhouette established in 1937 is still in vogue, with minor changes, 50 years later.

In the thirties and forties the new models were eagerly awaited every year. In those days, you were either a Ford man or a Chevrolet man. I for one was solidly in the Ford camp and I was mortified when the 1933 Ford, though it improved on the 1932 Graham's trend-setting lines, still had a rear end that was tucked in under the back seat instead of flaring out in line with the two rear fenders, as it did in the new Chevrolet. The Chevy also had a built-in trunk in some of its models, which was a triumph in both styling and utility. Two years later, however, Ford added a curving radiator shell, while Chevrolet clung to its old shell. There was progress indeed! I also remember wondering, in 1938, how the Lincoln Zephyr could possibly be improved. But it was: the running-boards were concealed under specially curved doors. What would they think of next? My older sister's fiancé, who was in the market for a car that year, refused to buy a Zephyr because it was too *avant-garde*.

There were, of course, mechanical improvements too. These were third-generation cars, and came after the early pioneering days as well as the period of technical consolidation that followed the First World War. Almost every year, during the thirties, brought significant improvements: first all-steel bodies, then hydraulic brakes, independent front suspension, synchromesh gears and later automatic transmissions, safety-glass windows and sealed-beam headlights.

This was the era of Swing, and inside even the cheapest cars looked like a living-room on wheels. Windowsills and instrument panels were invariably painted to look like hardwood, and some steering-wheels had spokes made of thick, chrome-plated wire that looked like the strings on a musical instrument. Car collectors today call them banjo wheels. Young bucks mounted "necking knobs" on them, so they could steer with one hand while using the other in more interesting ways.

Car ads of the time, though seldom as beautiful to look at as those of the twenties, provide a wonderful rearview-mirror glimpse of the habits and concerns of the day. Sexual and racial stereotypes were commonplace. Ordinary families driving ordinary cars have black servants —a fact which suggests that many of the ads were imported with little change from the US. It's always Father who is in the driver's seat, unless the advertiser has a station-wagon to sell, in which case the father of the family is driven to and from the commuter train by his faithful wife. "My husband knows all about engines and brakes," says a woman in a 1940 Ford ad, "but I'm the expert on style." "The salesman was grand," says another of Ford's women. "He never mentioned fan-belts or fuel-pumps or anything like that."

Then as now, reality was often quite different from what the ads proclaimed. You no longer see tire or car ads that boast of puncture-free service, but when a flat tire was still a common occurrence, manufacturers regularly boasted that their product was proof against blowouts. Cars were still sometimes made with not one but two spare tires, mounted in fender wells beside the hood. These were called sidemounts and are a desirable feature on the collectors' market to this day.

Nowhere do the advertisers hint of poverty or despair. Elegant couples in evening clothes cluster around new models, which were commonly made to look longer, wider and—oddly enough—higher than they really were. Cadillac may have claimed in 1932 that their cars were capable of "increased gasoline economy," but the savings the company offered were not intended for the landlord or the grocer. "Look at the lovely evening gown I bought," a satisfied customer is quoted as saying in 1937, "with what Dodge saved me in four months on gas alone!"

Perhaps the most striking thing about the cars built in Canada between 1932 and 1947 was their individuality. Today's cars look no

more unlike than a package of Kraft cheddar cheese and a package of Kraft mozzarella, but before the Second World War each make had a distinct personality of its own. Nobody could confuse the flashy Silver Streak Pontiac with the supremely elegant LaSalle, though both cars were made by General Motors and both had the same body shell. Nobody could possibly mistake the futuristic Airflow Chysler for the staid, aristocratic Packard.

They may not have been 100% Canadian, these *art-déco* cars with their V-shaped windshields, but they were built here and provided jobs for Canadian men and women, and that's more than can be said for many of the look-alike toy autos that clutter so many of our roads nowadays.

Free trade is fashionable in many circles in the mid-eighties, but the fact remains that our automobile industry—the No. 1 employer in the country—has grown and flourished in a climate of high tariffs. Today, the industry owes its existence to that unique and highly successful institution known as the auto pact. Perhaps what we need for the future is an auto pact with Japan.

THE PASSING SCENE

In 1932 Canada was in the depths of the depression. More than 25% of the work force was unemployed and a quarter of a million people were totally dependent on welfare, or the dole, as it was called at the time. Job-creation programs were inadequate and hindered by squabbling among the various levels of government. R. B. Bennett, the Prime Minister, who often sent a few dollars out of his own pocket to the poor, seemed unable to comprehend the enormity of the problem. He believed that the depression would be all over in a few months and refused to accept responsibility for developing solutions. Instead of financing make-work programs, his government cut the salaries of public servants and members of Parliament and increased sales, excise and income taxes. No wonder that, while delegates to the Imperial

The Pierce-Arrow Motor Company was established at Buffalo in 1901. Their cars had a long wheelbase (up to 139"), eight or twelve cylinders and cost about $3000. Only 189 of them were built in Canada. This is the 1933 model.

Economic Conference were being driven about Ottawa in a fleet of 50 bright new McLaughlin-Buicks, militant farmers and labourers in the West took it upon themselves to deal with the economic crisis. Together they founded the Co-operative Commonwealth Federation, headed by J.S. Woodsworth. In due course, the CCF became the NDP.

The 1932 cars all sported the smooth-brow look, with slanted windshields and rounded corners and no external sun visors. The most talked-about new models were the Ford V-8 and the fender-skirted Graham. The Graham was also notable as the first of that make to be manufactured in Canada, as were the 1932 Hudson and Pierce-Arrow. Durant and Reo merged as Dominion Motors and Studebaker introduced a low-priced six called the Rockne. The Hupmobile, which had not been made in Canada since before the First World War, reappeared as a Canadian-built vehicle with its 1932 model.

Things were no better in 1933. In that year there were 1.35 million Canadians on relief; 26.6% of the labour force was out of work and per-capita income fell to $247 per annum, off 48% in five years. To make matters worse, the federal government raised taxes once again.

One barrier to recovery was the high level of duties imposed on imported goods by both the United States and Canada. In April of 1933 the Prime Minister met Franklin D. Roosevelt in Washington, where he and the President agreed that tariffs should be lowered on both sides of the border, but the necessary legislation never got through the Congress.

Most of the 1933 models followed Graham's lead. They adopted deep-drawn fenders to hide the frame and many of them also sported heart-shaped radiator shells and long, flaring lines. After two years of disappointing sales, Studebaker dropped the Rockne. It was also the last year for the Canadian Willys and for the Frontenac, which is usually considered the last completely Canadian car.

If the thirties were the era of unemployment and poverty, they were also the era of glamour and romance. Greta Garbo was at the height of her career; young women smoked gold-tipped cigarettes and boys and girls danced cheek-to-cheek to the music of Guy Lombardo and his Royal Canadians.

The most exciting event of the year 1934 was the birth on 28 May of the Dionne quintuplets. Books are still being written about them. It was a medical first and the girls' survival was all the more remarkable in that there was no electricity in the farmhouse outside Callander, Ontario, where they were delivered by Dr. Allan Defoe. Together, the five babies weighed only $11\frac{1}{2}$ lbs. a week after their premature birth.

Unemployment was down in Canada in 1934 and this fact gave ground for renewed optimism about the future. The Bank of Canada was established and the City of Toronto celebrated its centennial.

Cars looked much the same in 1934 as they had the previous year. There were two notable exceptions. The Airflow Chrysler was a revolutionary vehicle in all respects, with its bridge-like body construction, its V-shaped windshield and its aerodynamic styling and waterfall grille. The new LaSalle, though less advanced in styling, was so sleek and svelte, with its long fenders and thin nose, that it made the futuristic Airflow look ungainly and old-fashioned. GM, for its part, introduced all-steel tops and a fully independent front-wheel suspension it called "knee-action."

In 1935 the Conservatives altered course. Bennett abandoned the remnants of his *laisser-faire* policy and, borrowing from Roosevelt's New Deal, came up with far-reaching proposals for social-security benefits, including unemployment insurance and regulated wages and hours of work. Not that the government hesitated to instruct the RCMP to disperse an On-to-Ottawa march by striking inmates of the hated relief camps. This decision led to a bloody confrontation at Regina in June. One policeman was killed and scores were injured on both sides.

Bennett's reform package was too little or too much, depending on whether you listened to the CCF or the Liberals. At anyrate, it was too late. There was a General Election on 14 October and the Conservatives lost by a wide margin. The Liberals, led by Mackenzie King, elected 173 members, the Conservatives only 40. Just two months before, Alberta voters had elected a Social Credit government under the premiership of William Aberhart, a man who liked to say that you didn't have to understand Social Credit before voting for him. After all, as he put it, do you have to wait until you understand electricity before turning on the lights? The Socreds elected seventeen members to the House of Commons in Ottawa that October.

In 1935 most of the new-model cars were restyled. Nearly all of them sported domed fenders instead of the bridal-gown sweep prevailing in previous years. Hupmobile developed an advanced body design with built-in headlights and a three-piece wrap-around windshield; Packard introduced its new, low-priced eight-cylinder Model 120. The last LaSalles and Pierce-Arrows to be made in Canada rolled off the assembly lines.

Mackenzie King lost no time in putting his

There's something very endearing about the girl's enthusiasm for the rather homely 1933 Essex Terraplane (below). The Terraplane was made by Hudson and, after only two years, in 1934, the Essex name was dropped. The company was one of the ancestors of the post-war American Motors.

"Isn't it a beauty, Ed? Mother's crazy about it, and I heard Father say it didn't cost a bit more than the ordinary low-priced sixes."

"Your father's as shrewd at car-buying as he is at crop-selling. Fred Waters down at the garage says these Terraplanes never need repair work."

The 1933 Frontenac, built by the Dominion Motors company of Leaside, Ontario, was the last automobile made exclusively in Canada. It was modeled on an American car, the Continental, and when the depression killed it, pro-

duction of the Frontenac also came to an end. Frontenac built a four as well as a six, and the four was said to deliver up to 37 miles per gallon. The last of the fours were sold new for as little as $595.

stamp on the country. He assembled a cabinet in nine days and less than a week later he was in Washington, where he persuaded Roosevelt to accept an arrangement whereby US tariffs were reduced on Canadian lumber, cattle and agricultural products in exchange for reduced duties on manufactured goods imported from the States. The duty on US cars came down from 30% to $17\frac{1}{2}$% before the end of 1936.

King closed the relief camps, but replaced them with a nationwide farm-placement scheme that offered the unemployed little more hope for the future. He was spared the bother of repealing the Conservatives' social-security legislation. The Supreme Court did that for him by declaring most of it invalid. In August, Maurice Duplessis and the Union Nationale brought the 40-year reign of the Liberals to an inglorious end in Quebec. Later in the same year, the CBC was set up.

Most of the 1936 cars were 1935 models, with minor changes. Two sensational *avant-garde* cars, the teardrop-shaped Lincoln Zephyr and the coffin-nosed Cord, made their *début* in the States, but neither was ever manufactured

The 1933 Willys, with its own distinctive brand of streamlining, was the last Willys built in this country. It was made by Willys-Overland of Toronto, another forebear of American Motors. The Hupp Motor Company of Windsor built Hupmobiles from 1910 until 1914 and again from 1931 until 1936. The model shown at right came out in 1935. Few images reveal as nakedly as this yesterday's vision of tomorrow.

in Canada. Nash started building cars at Windsor, Ontario, but after tariffs were reduced on cars imported from the United States, Cadillac and Studebaker both stopped making their products in Canada. Studebaker did not resume production in Canada until 1939; Cadillacs were never again made in this country. 1936 was also the last year for Reo and Hupmobile, in both Canada and the States, though the Hupmobile made a brief comeback south of the border a year or so later.

By 1937 the depression seemed to be coming to an end. But if corporate profits were higher, wages were not, and this fact led to conflicts between labour and management on a scale not seen in this country since the early twenties. There were 278 strikes and lockouts in 1937, involving 72,000 workers and resulting in a loss of 886,000 workdays. On top of that, the Prairie farmers, hit by drought, had their worst summer in history and, when the recovery faltered in the US in the fall, Canada was affected at once. Stocks fell once again, business activity dwindled and unemployment increased.

In April, however, Trans Canada Airlines (which became Air Canada in 1964) was established by act of Parliament. Its first commercial flight, from Vancouver to Seattle, took place on 1 September and six weeks later the airline began a regular scheduled service between Montreal and Vancouver. It carried mail and freight only; transcontinental passenger service did not begin until 1939.

Elegance was the common feature of the new cars for 1937. Chevrolet introduced a crease in the front door, foreshadowing the blending of fenders and bodies that was to come later. Ford borrowed the Lincoln Zephyr's pointed grille and Studebaker had a similar nose that incorporated the side louvres. Many cars had hoods that hinged at the rear.

In 1938, under pressure from his cabinet, Mackenzie King finally announced a program of public works and job training. Meanwhile, however, the provincial government in British Columbia had shut down the forestry camps that had replaced the farm-placement program for unemployed men and women. This left a lot of people without a place to live. On Bloody Sunday, 26 July, city police and RCMP officers used tear-gas and clubs on homeless protesters during a sit-in at the Vancouver post office. The riots that ensued came to an end only when the federal government offered free transportation to the protesters' home provinces.

In the automobile world styling changes were still *de rigueur*. If the 1937 models could

AIRFLOW CHRYSLER

THE MOST *Exciting*

be called feminine, the 1938 cars were masculine, with brutish grilles and big, boxy fenders. The new Buick boasted coil springs on all four wheels. Chrysler began building engines at Windsor for all its Canadian cars and trucks—until then they had been imported.

By and large, Canadians were not greatly concerned with events in Europe. Munich had come and gone. Canadians knew of Hitler's persecution of the Jews, but anti-Semitism was still not uncommon, not only in Quebec but in the rest of Canada as well. There were quotas restricting the entry of Jews into several of the professions; restrictive covenants were not unusual and many clubs and resorts were closed to Jews. What drew Canada into the war in 1939 was loyalty to Britain and the Commonwealth. Imperial pride had blossomed just a few months before during the royal tour, which is now remembered chiefly for the custom-built limousines, supplied by Chrysler, Packard, Lincoln and McLaughlin-Buick, that still dazzle crowds at parades today, almost 50 years later.

In August, the government pledged full support in case of war. On 10 September, a week after the British, Canada declared war on Germany. Before the year was out, a Canadian army division had arrived in the UK and the British Commonwealth Air Training Plan, which was to train some 130,000 aircrew from various countries, had been established.

The 1939 cars marked a return to softer lines again. The designers were apparently having trouble with noses and many were uncertain where to place the grille, vertically at the front of the hood or horizontally below the headlights or both. Chrysler, which opted for the waterfall nose, introduced a fluid coupling as an optional extra on the Imperial. Ford brought out a new medium-priced car, the Mercury. Studebaker added the Champion at the bottom of its price range and resumed production at Walkerville. It was the last year for the Canadian-built Packard.

Angered by opposition criticism, Mackenzie King called a snap election for 26 March, 1940 and was returned to power in a convincing victory with 53% of the popular vote. In June,

Car IN YEARS......

The buying public, as it turned out, wasn't ready for the visual and mechanical improvements offered by Chrysler in its 1934 Airflow (above). It was the biggest failure ever endured by the industry until the appearance of the Edsel a generation later. The 1934 Ford (overleaf) despite its low price, was one of the most graceful cars of the year. It differed from the 1933 model in that the side louvres were straight instead of curved. Ford is the oldest surviving car-maker in Canada. The company opened in Walkerville in 1904. Chrysler didn't start building cars in this country until 1925.

after the fall of France and the Low Countries, the National Resources Mobilization Act put Canada on a war footing for the first time. Registration of all adults began in August and conscription for home service followed in October. For the time being, King refrained from asking for the authority to send conscripts overseas.

On 18 August, at an historic meeting held in Ogdensburg, New York, King and Roosevelt agreed to set up a Permanent Joint Board of Defence, a move that took Canada out of the British and into the American sphere of influence. Many facets of life, from the right to price a product as you wished to the right to seek the job of your choice, were now subject to government control. Under the forceful direction of the Minister of Munitions and Supplies, C. D. Howe, Canada became a major supplier of materiel to the Allied forces.

Surprisingly enough, the production of cars for civilian use continued unabated. Bodies were wider and lower, all cars had built-in headlights and gear-shift levers were moved from the floor to the steering-wheel. The new Oldsmobile was equipped with Hydramatic transmission. 1940 was, however, the last year of the Graham, both in Canada and the United States.

By the middle of 1941 there were 25,000 Canadian Army volunteers overseas; thousands of Canadians were taking the war to the enemy in the service of the RCAF and the RAF; and the Royal Canadian Navy was playing a major role in the Battle of the Atlantic.

The government increased taxes once again, froze prices and wages, created the Canadian Women's Army Corps and outlawed the Communist Party. In April, King and Roosevelt met again and signed the Hyde Park Agreement, under which Canadian purchases of American components for use in munitions destined for Britain would be charged to Britain under the Lend-Lease program. This agreement enabled Canada to develop its manufacturing industries much more rapidly than would otherwise have been possible. By the end of the war, Canada had become the fourth-largest Allied supplier of war materials.

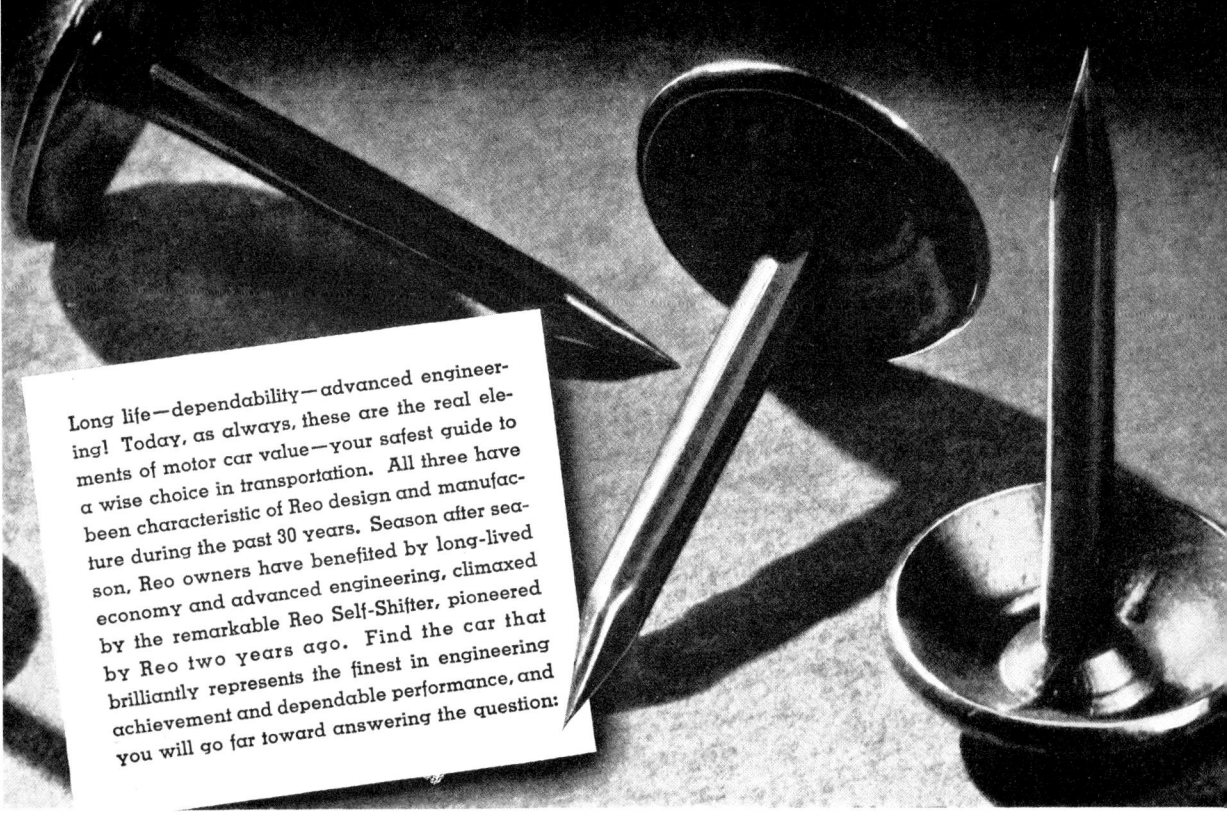

LET'S GET DOWN TO BRASS TACK

Long life—dependability—advanced engineering! Today, as always, these are the real elements of motor car value—your safest guide to a wise choice in transportation. All three have been characteristic of Reo design and manufacture during the past 30 years. Season after season, Reo owners have benefited by long-lived economy and advanced engineering, climaxed by the remarkable Reo Self-Shifter, pioneered by Reo two years ago. Find the car that brilliantly represents the finest in engineering achievement and dependable performance, and you will go far toward answering the question:

On 7 December, 1941, the day of the attack on Pearl Harbor, Canada declared war on Japan —24 hours before the United States took the same step. It was later that month, while addressing Parliament in Ottawa, that Winston Churchill made his famous boast. Referring to Hitler's claim that he would wring England's neck like a chicken, Churchill retorted, "Some chicken! Some neck!"

Though more and more companies were retooling for war production, Canada built more than 96,000 passenger cars in 1941—fewer than in 1937, when production reached almost 133,000 units, but more than in 1939, when only 90,00 cars were made. Naturally enough, commercial vehicles were given priority and no fewer than 173,600 were built. In 1941, cars

were generally wider than before. Runningboards disappeared behind the doors on most models. Hudson ceased civilian production al-

THE 1935 CADILLAC

Reo cars were made in small quantities in Toronto and Leaside between 1931 and 1935. The 1935 model (left) was equipped with automatic transmission. That year even Cadillac (above) cut its prices.

together and no Hudson cars were made in this country until 1950.

1942: this was the year Japanese-Canadians were evacuated from the West Coast, the year of the national plebiscite on conscription for overseas service, the year of the disaster on the beaches of Dieppe.

The evacuation of people of Japanese extraction to the interior began in February and eventually over 19,000 were affected. The plebiscite was held in April and Canadians in every province except Quebec voted Yes. Mackenzie King, anxious to preserve national unity, promised not to send draftees overseas unless and until it was absolutely necessary. In August,

In 1936, Chevrolet (above) had its best year since 1929. It had hydraulic brakes and fully independent front-wheel suspension. With its all-steel top, it was billed as "the only complete car" in the low-price field. The austere lines of the 1935 Dodge (right) look strangely out of place in this setting. Dodge began making cars in Walkerville in 1924.

"COSTS LESS TO RUN THAN ANY CAR I EVER OWNED!" SAY OWNERS OF NEW-VALUE DODGE

Dodge economy startles America! Owners report, "We get 20 to 24 miles on a gallon of gas... save 30¢ to 40¢ on every dollar's worth of oil!"

ACTUAL driving experience in the hands of thousands of owners† *proves* the New-Value Dodge is America's most economical car. Not only cheaper to run than cars at or above its price... but reports of users show Dodge positively costs less for gas and oil than even the small cars! Yet, to get this sensational Dodge economy you don't have to sacrifice style, bigness or riding comfort. Far from it! Dodge has size, luxury, rich appointments. Dodge gives you the new "Airglide Ride"... new "Synchromatic Control" that makes driving almost effortless... time-tested Dodge dual-cylinder hydraulic brakes... Dodge perfected all-steel body... 95 major advancements! The result of Dodge's 20 years' experience in building almost three million fine vehicles. Remember, Dodge delivers for just a few dollars more than lowest-priced cars.

†*Owners' letters in our files.*

THE *Airglide* RIDE

1. Dodge "Levelator" and new multi-leaf springs give "Airglide Ride"—check body roll and sidesway.
2. "Red Ram" engine moved forward 8 inches to permit equal distribution of weight on all 4 wheels.
3. Floor lowered 3½ inches to give seats the height of a comfortable living-room chair.
4. Rear seat moved forward 6 inches. Passengers seated ahead of axle "shock-line".

"SMART AS TOMORROW"—On looks alone, Dodge is the "more-for-your-money" car. It is smarter... and it is more economical... safer... more dependable! Yet delivers for just a few dollars more than lowest-priced cars.

NEW INTERIOR LUXURY—The smartness of this new-value Dodge interior is rivaled only by its unusual roominess and luxurious comfort.

"THRILLING ECONOMY"—There's a real thrill to the economy of Dodge ownership. Every time you check up on gas and oil you find you're saving money!... Saving not merely pennies but dollars!

NO SIDESWAY—New "Levelator" tends to keep Dodge on an even keel. Checks sidesway even on sharp turns... hugs the road. New comfort and new safety for you!

New-Value DODGE NOW ONLY $645*

NEW-VALUE DODGE: Coupe $645, 2-door Sedan $690, Rumble Seat Coupe $710, Touring Sedan (2-door, with built-in trunk) $715, Sedan $735, Touring Sedan (4-door, with built-in trunk) $760. *All prices f. o. b. factory, Detroit, subject to change without notice. Special equipment extra. Time payments to fit your budget. Ask for the official Chrysler Motors Commercial Credit Plan.

DELIVERS NOW FOR JUST A FEW DOLLARS MORE THAN LOWEST-PRICED CARS

"No, I don't run a dress-shop, manage a tea-room or go to an office. I'm just a wife." This sort of thing didn't raise an eyebrow in 1936 when Packard added the low-priced six-cylinder model shown above to its product line. Packards were made at Windsor until 1939. Ford had a similar view of women and offered their V-8 as *"an exceptionally good choice for the woman motorist because it is so dependable and easy to handle."* In the ad reproduced at right even the geese fly in a V-8 formation. The four-door (or Fordor, as Ford called it, not to be mistaken for the two-door Tudor) convertible sedan shown here is now one of the most sought-after models of its period.

"ALL these Hudso

In the whole moderate price field, only Hudson owners can tell you how much easier, safer and more enjoyable it is to drive with the Selective Automatic Shift. Shifting gears with the flick of a finger at the steering wheel ... and a lift of the toe from the accelerator. Never pulling a gear lever or touching a clutch pedal. Yet *nothing new to learn!* With all the extra roominess of a *clear* floor in front. Selective Automatic Shift is an optional extra on all 1937 Hudsons ... conventional gear shift available without cost if wanted.

No. 1 CAR OF THE MODERATE PRICE FIELD

The bulky 1937 Hudson (above) was perhaps the ultimate expression of the melting-brick-of-ice-cream school of design. The new Hudsons dispensed with the clutch-pedal and, as an optional extra, had the gear-shift lever mounted on the steering-column. Hudson boasted leaf springs on all four wheels, the finest of interior fabrics and, for customers with an eye to economy, the ability to deliver 28.39 miles to the Imperial gallon, with five passengers and their luggage, "and no coasting." Hudsons were made in Canada from 1932 until 1957.

almost 1000 Canadians were killed and twice that many taken prisoner in the raid on Dieppe. At home, gasoline and butter were rationed. Canada broke off diplomatic relations with the Vichy government in France. The Alaska Highway, giving Alaska its first road link with the continental United States, was completed.

The 1942 cars were 1941 models with cosmetic changes. Most of them had been built in the previous year, as the production of cars for civilian use ceased in both Canada and the US early in the new year. The only innovative cars were supplied by General Motors: Buick, Cadillac and Oldsmobile all had new, wider bodies.

On 19 January, 1943 Ottawa people were surprised to see a foreign flag flying from the Peace Tower—something that had never happened before or since. It was the Royal Standard of the House of Orange, hoisted in honour of the birth of Margriet, third daughter of Princess Juliana of the Netherlands, who was living in exile in Canada. Later in the year, Canada became a member of the Combined Food Board, which gave her, as an important producer of foodstuffs, an increased voice in Allied decision-making. Production of war materials was now at its peak, with a value of over $2 billion in 1943 alone. Vehicle production reached a level of 4000 units a week.

The war news improved in 1944, but the cost was great. In the first months after the Allied invasion of Europe on 6 June, casualties among Canadian ground forces numbered over 30,000. King felt obliged to draft 16,000 men for overseas duty, but most of them never left the country.

On 15 June the CCF under Tommy Douglas won in Saskatchewan and formed the first socialist government ever to be elected in North America.

The war in Europe ended on 8 May, 1945. Canadian casualties totalled over 42,000, but the sustained production of materiel had been good for the economy. The GNP had more than doubled and in 1945 stood at $11.8 billion. Since 1939 there had been no appreciable rise

Except for the outside horns, this 1937 Graham is typical of its year.

in the cost of living.

There was a general election in June in which the Liberals were returned to power despite the loss of 65 seats. Meat and butter were both still rationed and price and wage controls stayed in place. In July the first baby bonuses were sent out. Two months later Igor Gouzenko, a cipher clerk at the Soviet Embassy in Ottawa, came to the offices of the Ottawa *Journal* and told reporters of a spy ring that had been operating in Canada all through the war. His revelations shook the capitals of he world and led to much stricter security measures in all the Western countries.

At last automakers began to advertise new cars. Ford kicked off a campaign announcing that "there's a Ford in your future!"

The biggest news of 1946 came as a direct result of Gouzenko's disclosures. In February, after a pre-dawn raid in Ottawa, some twenty present and former public servants, all of them Canadian, were arrested on charges of having disclosed secret information to "a foreign mission." Eventually ten of them, including a member of Parliament, were convicted. Undeterred by the conservative backlash against "liberal" thinking, Tommy Douglas introduced a program of universal hospital insurance in the province of Saskatchewan.

The 1946 cars—which were nothing but updated 1942 models—were eagerly bought up by a car-hungry public. The GM models all had fenders extending partway into the body. Some of the pre-war makes, such as Hupmobile,

This 1937 McLaughlin-Buick sold for $1207.

This is the Nash-LaFayette four-door sedan, a good example of 1937 styling at its best. Nash introduced the first seamless all-steel body, but in advertisements its makers concentrated on the claim that their car was roomier and more comfortable than other cars in its price-range. Nash opened for business in Windsor in 1936 and merged with Hudson to form American Motors in 1954. The LaFayette was first made in 1934 and was discontinued in 1939.

The new 1938 Packard Eight

The 1938 Packard illustrated above is the car in Anton Myrer's bestseller, "The Last Convertible." It was a finely-made conveyance with a solid feel and the looks of a bank-vault. In 1941 Chrysler was still using the term Airflow and their new Fluid Drive transmission was said to deliver "the power of Niagara" with the smoothness of a turbine. Diagrams were provided to show how the miracle was accomplished.

LaSalle, Pierce-Arrow and the Reo passenger car, were gone forever, but Canada had two new cars: the Mercury 114, a low-priced model, and the Monarch, a twin of the Mercury, for sale, unlike the Mercury (for which a Mercury dealership was required) by all Ford dealers.

Inflation and a heavy negative trade balance with the United States led to import restrictions in 1947. Price ceilings on certain foodstuffs were reimposed, but then in November all economic controls, including food rationing but excluding the regulation of rents, were lifted. In February huge reserves of oil had been discovered at Leduc, Alberta.

Most of the new cars differed from the 1946 models in trim only, but there were three important exceptions: Kaiser, Frazer and Studebaker. The first two were newcomers to the market but were never produced in Canada; the Studebaker was the first Canadian post-war model of that make.

What the three cars had in common was that

The 1938 Pontiac had the massive look that was de rigueur that year, but the drawing above shows that the designers were capable of an imaginative treatment of the grille and louvres. Beauty and luxury were given top billing. The mechanical improvements— increased generator capacity, a new waterpump, sealed bearings—were of minor importance. Pontiacs have been made in Canada since 1926. Plymouth began production here two years later. The 1938 model shown at left was a solid, comfortable car, but its styling was awkward. The silhouette was high and full of lines with nowhere to go.

the front fenders had been completely integrated into the body; in the case of the Kaiser and the Frazer, the rear fenders were handled in the same way. Within two years all makes had followed suit, making this as radical and sweeping a revolution in style as the introduction of the Graham fender in 1932. Gone forever were external headlights, running-boards, spare wheels and fenders. It was all a single unit from now on. The automobile had at last assumed its mature form.

ONE FOR THE ROAD

Where are they now, these splendid vehicles of half a century ago? Some, as we have seen, were wilfully destroyed under the GM Used Car Disposal Plan, but thousands of them are still alive and running. Most are in the hands of antique-car lovers, many of whom have taken their cars apart and painstakingly restored them to their original condition. These patient men have in a very practical and concrete way contributed to the preservation of an important part of Canadian history.

But the old-car hobby is not for everyone. It's a most satisfying pastime for anyone with a mechanical bent who likes to skin his knuckles on vintage valves. But for those of us who lack this talent (or the inclination to acquire it), antique cars are a poor investment, financially as well as emotionally. Few things can spoil a day more quickly than a car that stalls in the middle of traffic for no apparent reason, and if you hardly know the difference between a carburetor and a radiator, there's always one thing you do know: it's going to cost you plenty to have it fixed.

Fortunately, however, the cars of the thirties and forties are easier to repair than most. They are not as exotic and unorthodox as the earliest models, nor as complicated as the contemporary automobile. They're ideal for the determined hobbyist.

The strange thing about vintage cars is that there seems to be no way to explain the fluctuations in their market value. One would think,

This is the first Mercury—the 1939 model. Its rounded outline was characteristic of all the Fords built in Canada until 1948. The Mercury was intended to give the company a mid-priced car that would attract buyers who wanted something more luxurious than the Ford V-8 but could not afford the Lincoln at the top of the line. The Mercury is still built in Canada.

"I had no idea the Ford was such a nice car!"

Ginger Rogers, who could afford any car, drove a 1939 DeSoto (left). The implications are obvious, even today. The DeSoto was made in this country from 1931 till 1960. The 1939 Fordor sedan (above) had an interior fitted with imitation wood—a "deluxe surprise."

for example, that such milestone cars as the 1947 Studebaker would be more valuable today than, say, an ordinary Ford sedan of the mid-thirties. The opposite, however, is often true.

In the State of Washington this year there was a 1947 two-door Studebaker for sale for $695 US. One must assume it was badly in need of restoration. In California, at about the same time, someone was offering a 1948 Ford two-

door, a "great candidate for restoration," for $3200 US. In Kansas not long ago there was a 1947 Studebaker Champion convertible (a very rare body style of a very rare car), completely restored to mint condition, for sale at $9700 US. A Ford convertible of the same year and in the same condition—of which there is a plentiful supply—would cost some $15,000 US; the same model in a 1935 or 1936 version would cost at least $25,000 US.

If you can afford the going prices, there are some very rare and desirable cars on the market. In Arkansas not long ago a 1932 Graham 8 (the trail-blazing model with the first fender

Nash made cars at Windsor from 1936 until 1957. The 1940 model (above) had back seats that could be made up into a bed for overnight camping. The 1940 Pontiac (facing page) was really a Chevrolet in disguise. The two cars had the same motor, wheelbase and body shell.

A CREDIT TO YOUR PURSE

..a Credit to your Judgment, too

YOU CAN'T BLAME *anybody* for buying a 1940 Pontiac on the basis of *beauty alone*. It's the *most beautiful thing on wheels*. But once you've owned one of these big silver streaked beauties, you make the pleasant discovery that buying a Pontiac isn't only evidence of good taste. It's *right in line* with your purse... *right in line* with your good judgment, too!

There's 27 striking new models—and *prices start with the lowest*. But you get so much *extra* comfort, *extra* performance, *extra* luxury, *extra* quality and EXTRA SATISFACTION — that you'll be apt to call Pontiac the best investment you ever made. Check your Pontiac dealer — *and see if that isn't true*.

Pontiac engineers were first to introduce the steering wheel shift, that outstanding contribution to handling ease which practically every manufacturer has since adopted.

For 1940, 27 Brilliant New Models. 5 New Series: Pontiac "Arrow" Six (Standard and De Luxe); Pontiac "Special" Six; Pontiac De Luxe Six; Pontiac De Luxe Eight; Pontiac "Torpedo" Eight.

FOR PRIDE AND PERFORMANCE

As late as 1941, Chevrolet made no apology for retaining running-boards, concealed though they were by a curving door-jamb. By now, of course, drivers could put the top up or down at the touch of a button. Studebaker entered the low-priced field in 1939 with the Champion. The 1940 model (facing page) cost only $919 at the factory in Walkerville, where Studebakers were made from 1912 until 1936 and again from 1939 until 1941. After the war, production was resumed at a new plant in Hamilton.

Illustrated above: 1940 Studebaker Champion Club Sedan $977 delivered at factory

Thrilling beauty and welcome money-saving make you proud to say you own this

1940 STUDEBAKER CHAMPION

Delightful comfort in zero weather is yours with Studebaker's Climatizer which warms entire car, including floor, with filtered, heated, constantly changing, fresh air—defrosts and defogs, too. Entire Climatizer unit is located out of the way under front seat. Available at slight extra cost.

You don't need to slam the doors of your Champion, thanks to Studebaker's tight-closing rotary door latches. Solid steel body, foot-regulated hydraulic brakes and sealed-beam headlamps contribute still further to your safety.

YOU'RE doing the same up-to-the-minute thinking as thousands of other experienced motorists, when you choose this beautiful new Studebaker Champion as the best buy in a lowest price car.

The biggest boosters among the Champion's owners are men and women who have driven other cars of lowest price. They enthusiastically say they never dreamed that any car could give so much downright satisfaction in looks, safety, riding comfort, handling ease, smooth performance and economy as this Champion.

Costs 10% to 25% less to run

Studebaker engineers designed the Champion to be 10% to 25% more saving of gas than any other leading lowest price car. Many Champion owners get even better gas economy.

This roomy, luxuriously upholstered, 6-cylinder Studebaker saves you money on repairs and upkeep, too, because it is built with the same care and soundness as Studebaker's famed Commander and President.

At no extra cost, you get such conveniences and protections as planar independent suspension, finest hydraulic shock absorbers, steering wheel gear shift, sealed-beam headlamps, non-slam rotary door latches, front-compartment hood lock, shockless variable-ratio steering, foot-regulated hydraulic brakes.

See your local Studebaker dealer now. Become the proud owner of a Studebaker Champion. Easy terms.

PRICES BEGIN AT $919

for Champion coupe delivered at Walkerville. All prices subject to change without notice.

STUDEBAKER BEATS ALL OTHER CARS in official gas economy classic!

★

CHAMPION AVERAGES 35.03 MILES PER IMP. GAL.

Studebaker cars, with low-extra-cost overdrive, finished 1—2—3 in the Gilmore-Yosemite Sweepstakes, ahead of 25 cars of all prices and sizes. The Studebaker Champion, with an official 35.03 miles per Imperial gallon, proved itself 17% to 29% superior in gas economy to the 3 other large-selling low price cars.

Advertisements for the 1941 Plymouth made the most of a car that had little to commend it. The new cars were almost identical to those of the previous year. The car's best features were its excellent brakes and comfortable, chair-high seats. The makers claimed to have made nineteen major improvements, but gave few details.

*Civilian automobile production ceased
early in 1942 and cars like the 1942
Mercury (above) are now extremely rare
and highly prized by collectors.
At the time, the 1942 models seemed
to have little to add
to those of the year before.*

Mercury 8

Concealed headlights—like those on the 1936 Cord—distinguished the 1942 DeSoto. The stylized, distorted artwork, making much of the prominent, aggressive grille, recalls a different time when bigger was better.

More than half of the military vehicles produced in Canada during the Second World War were Fords. In the 1944 ad above Ford cars are shown at work at home and at the front. They carried chiefs of staff to the scene of action; meanwhile, men employed in war production could count on Ford cars to get them to work. General Motors called its 1943 models, which included military vehicles of every sort, Models for Victory. Five are pictured at right.

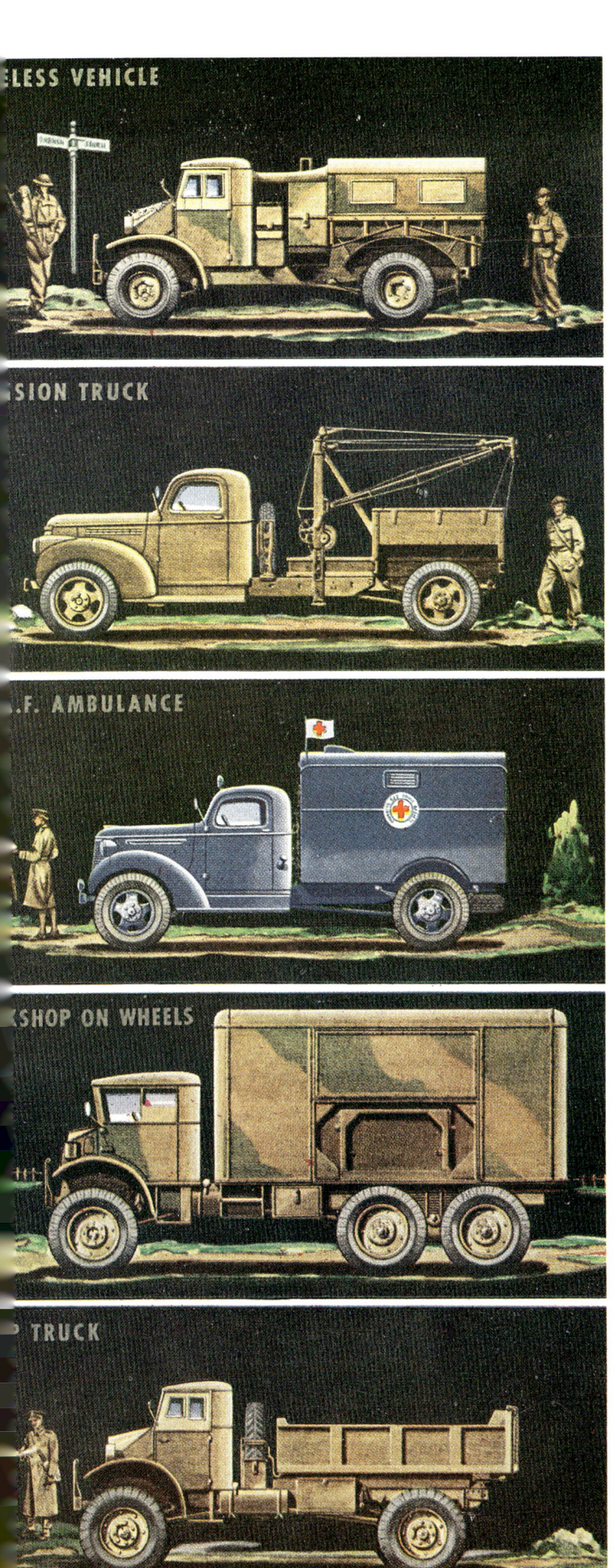

It took some time for the post-war models to reach the dealers. The DeSoto ad reproduced at left appeared in the fall of 1945, but the car is a 1942 model. The concealed headlights disappeared after the war. The 1946 Oldsmobile (above) had the same body as the Buick of that year. Note the front fenders, which flow across the doors. Similar styling persisted on both cars, with minor changes, until 1948.

YOUR EYES are windows

Just frame it in the picture window of your eye. Drive it for the pleasant world it offers. Own it because it is a perfect woman's car, as half a million husbands know.

It is all-fluid driven for your ease and comfort.

Its brakes are extra-powered for your security. Its style and trim are as rich and fine as your own good taste.

Dodge

SMOOTHEST CAR "AFLOAT"
Lowest Priced Car with Fluid Drive

skirts) with dual sidemounts and in "unbelievably nice original condition" was offered for $12,500 US or best offer. In Tennessee at about the same time there was a seldom-seen 1935 Hupmobile, the one with the three-piece wraparound windshield, restored in 1980, for the same price.

It's often cheaper to buy a car in Canada, if the one you want is to be found anywhere near where you live. For those who don't insist on a restored specimen, or who prefer to do the restoration themselves, Finn Eriksen of Victoria, BC had a huge 1941 Buick Special four-door slant-back sedan, complete and running, for

In the car-starved years immediately after the war, a scene like that on the facing page could only have whetted the appetites of thousands of readers. Picture-windows were new then and so was the exhilaration of buying a new car for the first time in five years. The 1947 Studebaker (above) was designed by Raymond Loewy and was the first car to integrate the fenders and the body. The five-passenger coupé had the first one-piece curved windshield ever made.

The 1947 Monarch, which was identical to the Mercury, was never made in the United States. It was intended to give Ford dealers a medium-priced car to sell and was introduced, in Canada, the year before. It was an immediate success.

sale last year for only $2500 Canadian. In Montmagny, Quebec, Michel Ouellet was offering a 1933 Ford coupé with a rumble-seat, in need of restoration, for $2750 and in Montreal Bob Modugno had a beautiful 1940 Ford convertible, recently restored, for sale for $10,900.

But what the old-car hobby needs, even more than money, is a handy tinkerer who is willing to spend an enormous amount of time in restoring the ordinary cars that are usually overlooked by the connoisseurs and the museum curators. Surely these workaday coupés and sedans that made the town and country what they were during the thirties and forties are a heritage that is worth preserving, even at considerable cost, for future generations.

FOURTEEN DAYS